CAN I TELL
YOU ABOUT
GENDER
DIVERSITY?

CAN I TELL YOU ABOUT...?

The 'Can I tell you about...?' series offers simple introductions to a range of limiting conditions and other issues that affect our lives. Friendly characters invite readers to learn about their experiences, the challenges they face, and how they would like to be helped and supported. These books serve as excellent starting points for family and classroom discussions.

Other subjects covered in the Can I tell you about...? series

ADHD

Adoption

Anxiety

Asperger Syndrome

Asthma

Autism

Cerebral Palsy

Dementia

Depression

Diabetes (Type 1)

Down Syndrome

Dyslexia

Dyspraxia

Eating Disorders

Eczema

Epilepsy

ME/Chronic Fatigue
    Syndrome

Multiple Sclerosis

OCD

Parkinson's Disease

Pathological Demand
Avoidance Syndrome

Peanut Allergy

Selective Mutism

Sensory Processing
Difficulties

Stammering/Stuttering

Stroke

Tourette Syndrome

CAN I TELL YOU ABOUT
GENDER DIVERSITY?

A guide for friends, family and professionals

CJ ATKINSON
Illustrated by Olly Pike

Jessica Kingsley *Publishers*
London and Philadelphia

First published in 2017
by Jessica Kingsley Publishers
73 Collier Street
London N1 9BE, UK
and
400 Market Street, Suite 400
Philadelphia, PA 19106, USA

www.jkp.com

Library of Congress Cataloging in Publication Data
A CIP catalog record for this book is available
from the Library of Congress

British Library Cataloguing in Publication Data
A CIP catalogue record for this book is
available from the British Library

ISBN 978 1 78592 105 6
eISBN 978 1 78450 367 3

Printed and bound in Great Britain

CONTENTS

"My name is Kit and I'm 12 years old. I live in a house with my mum and dad, and our dog, Pickle.

When I was born, the doctors told my mum and dad that they had a baby girl, and so for the first few years of my life that's how my parents raised me. This is called being assigned female at birth. I wasn't ever very happy that way. I didn't like playing with dolls, or wearing dresses, and I hated having long hair. My mum remembers that when I was three I asked everybody to call me Christopher. Any time somebody called me a girl, I would say no, *boy*.

This got really hard when I started school. That's when I would get into trouble for sitting with the boys, or not doing 'girl' things. My mum and dad had always just let me play however I wanted, and now that wasn't really allowed as much.

One time in my English class, I wrote a story about a girl who wanted to grow up to be a prince and not a princess. She didn't want to wear fancy dresses or go to a ball, but instead wanted to grow up to have a suit of armour, and a horse, and for everyone to call her Sir. Everybody told her that she had to be a princess and there was nothing she could do about it. She was so sad, and when I had to read the story out in class I started to cry because I knew exactly what the princess was going through. I knew because all I wanted was to be a prince, but it was like everybody was telling me that I had to want to grow up to be a princess.

That was when my teacher asked if everything was okay at home, or if I needed some help or somebody to talk to. I told him all about how it felt on the inside, how girl things just made me feel confused and worried but boy things made me happy. How all I really wanted to do was to cut my hair and have people realise that I was a boy. The teacher asked my parents to come in and have a talk, and I got to tell them what was happening in my head.

My mum and dad were a little bit surprised but they hugged me really hard and said that they would do anything to help me because they only cared about me being happy, and the minute they said that I stopped feeling worried and sad – it was like I could actually take a really deep breath of air!"

"You see, I have a different gender identity than I was assigned at birth. Another name for this is called being transgender. For some people, this is like feeling as though you are born in the wrong body, or like the body that you have doesn't match how you feel in your head. This can happen to people who were assigned female at birth, male at birth, or those who are intersex.

Some people are born with body chemistry that isn't 'typical' for a girl or a boy. This happens with about one in every 2000 people that are born, and is called being intersex. Some intersex people identify as transgender, and some don't.

Other people never have any confusion about their gender from when they are born. They feel like how the world sees them and how they see themselves are the same. This is called being cisgender.

Not everybody realises these things at the same time in their lives. I knew my whole life that there was something that wasn't right, and I didn't want to be called a girl. Sometimes it takes until a person is going through puberty, when their bodies are changing and that when they realise that things aren't feeling right for them at all. Other people don't realise until they're an adult, or until a little bit later in their lives. This doesn't mean that they're any less trans or that they are going through any less, it's just that some people go through different things at different times.

Some trans people are binary – they feel like they were born in the wrong body, and that they are the opposite gender. Non-binary people don't feel like this at all. They may not feel anything like male or female, or they might feel every part of male and female. They may have different identities, or it might change. Some non-binary people identify as transgender and some don't. It can be confusing, but it helps if you start to think about gender as different from, say, a light switch, and a bit more like a spectrum. Instead of people only being able to be a boy or a girl, some people might fall anywhere in between. When we talk about somebody being only a boy or a girl, we call this being binary.

When it comes to talking to people who identify differently, it's really important not to make assumptions, and to listen to what the person tells you about who they are. After all, they know themselves better than you do! That's the great thing about a spectrum – you can be at either end of it, or you can fall somewhere in the middle, and nobody has to feel left out.

The main thing to remember about a spectrum is that it's like a sliding scale, but nobody is better than anybody else. If somebody is trans, then they are trans. There's no such thing in the world as not being trans enough, and it's not for anybody else to decide who or what you are. If a person chooses not to medically transition, that doesn't make them less trans. What a person chooses to do with their own body doesn't make them more or less of a person!"

"One of the ways that people get confused about trans people is that they think it has anything to do with being gay. Another word for gay is homosexual, and that doesn't have anything to do with your gender but instead has to do with the people that you are attracted to.

Homosexuals are people who like people who are the same gender that they are. Women who like women are called lesbians, and men who like men are called gay. These words are scary to some people, which is silly. Bisexual and pansexual people are attracted to any gender. Asexual people simply don't experience sexual attraction to people.

Just like gender identity, sexual orientation can be a bit of a spectrum. Some people might see themselves as 100% heterosexual or 100% homosexual. Other people might change as they get older, or depending on the people that they meet in their lives.

Just like cisgender people, trans people can be straight, or gay, or bisexual, or asexual. Sometimes this might change as people go through transition and become more comfortable with themselves. That's the other great thing about a spectrum – it might not always be the same every day of your life. This doesn't have to be scary at all."

"When you start to live as the gender you identify as, this is called transitioning. There are some different kinds of transition.

When I asked people to start calling me Kit, and using he/him pronouns, this is called social transition. It means that everybody in my life knows who I am, and treats me the way they'd treat any other boy. I wear boy's clothes, and I have a boy's hair cut, and people refer to me as he/him. This is a big step for trans people, as it can be the first time in our lives that the world really acknowledges us for who we are.

This is a step that my mum and dad found hard at first. We talked about the name that I would take and we decided that Kit suited me. They also helped me change my name officially, which is another big part of transition. We changed the name on my birth certificate, and we told the school all about what I was going through so that all of my records would be up to date. When I applied for my first passport, it was really exciting because it came in my real name!

Then there's medical transition. This is when somebody goes to the doctor for help. Some trans people do this, and some don't, and it doesn't change how trans you are if you do or don't.

Medical transition for people my age is usually hormone blockers. These stop me from going through female puberty, and stop my body developing in ways that make me unhappy. When I'm 18, I'll be allowed to go onto hormone replacement therapy – this means that I'll start to develop facial hair, and my body will go through boy puberty. If I don't want to do this, I can stop taking hormone blockers because they are reversible.

Some people also decide that they would like surgery, to help their bodies feel right. This can involve lots of different things to help you, but you cannot have surgery until you've turned at least 18. One of the things about medical transition is that it takes a long, long time, which can be really good for making sure you know your own mind, but also really hard, because it involves a lot of waiting around.

This is something I found really difficult, and made me sad a lot. It's like you're always waiting around for something to happen."

"One of the ways that people start to get comfortable with themselves is by experimenting with their gender expression. This means looking at what you wear and how you style your hair, and looking at the things that the world says are for girls and boys. For a lot of people this is how they start to socially transition.

We all know that pink and blue are just colours, and that they don't mean anything at all, but because of the way the world is built, a lot of boy things are blue and a lot of girl things are pink. This means for some people, it can be the easiest way for people to experiment with their gender expression – by playing with different coloured toys, or dolls, or clothes. When I was little, I never wanted anything pink, and everybody said that I was a little tomboy and that one day I'd grow out of it.

Obviously girls can wear trousers, and boys can like the colour pink. My best friend Lana is a cisgender girl. She has long dark hair and likes to wear tutus, and her favourite things to do are to read and to climb trees. Sometimes she likes to do 'boy' things like play football and she's always really competitive, but nobody worries about whether or not she is a girl. Sometimes she acts like a boy, but it's different for her than it is for me because Lana's happy being a girl, just sometimes she wants to do boy things. My mum says this is because there's no such thing as boy things and girl things, there are just things and that we shouldn't worry too much about it if it makes us happy. I just know that in my insides I'm a boy doing things, just like Lana knows that she's a girl doing things.

You cannot tell if somebody is transgender just by looking at them. A boy might have long hair and wear skirts and still be a happy boy.

A girl might have short hair for the same reason anybody might have short hair – because she thinks she looks nice.

One of the things that people say a lot is that transgender kids will grow out of it. When people say this to me it makes me sad, because I know that they don't really understand what it means to be trans. They think that because they've never felt like this in their bodies that nobody can.

Something that has really helped me has been looking at all the videos that people put up on YouTube. There are lots of boys and girls and non-binary people who make videos every day talking about what their bodies mean to them, and how they feel about their gender. It's really important to have creative things like this, especially when you're not feeling happy in your body, because it gives you the chance to feel heard and understood."

"How you look and how you behave might have nothing to do with being transgender or everything to do with it. Being transgender is about feeling that your gender identity is anything other than how you were assigned at birth. One of the ways that people can become really aware of this is because they have gender dysphoria.

Gender dysphoria is really hard to explain because it's not the same for everybody. For me, it feels like being really really uncomfortable in my body. I don't like to look in the mirror, or when I'm taking a shower I make sure I don't look at my body. Sometimes I feel like my body isn't my body but a body that belongs to somebody else, and it's felt like this all of my life.

My friend Amy, who I met at the clinic, didn't really start to feel dysphoric until she was 12 and her body started changing in a way that made her feel really bad about herself. That happens for people a lot, when your body changes and you realise you don't want it to change in a certain way. Her body was changing in ways that made her miserable, and she got really depressed. It can be so scary to feel these things and not have anybody to talk to or anybody who can understand you.

A lot of people who have gender dysphoria go to the doctors because they need help to feel more comfortable in their own bodies, but not every trans person will experience gender dysphoria, just like not every trans person will go to the doctors and go through medical transition.

Some people experience something called gender euphoria. This is where somebody recognises you as the gender you feel, and makes you really great about yourself. For some people, being trans can be really scary and upsetting, but for other people it's about feeling joyful and excited about getting to be your truest self. There really isn't one particular way to be trans, and people have to find what works best for them."

"A fter I told my mum and dad what was happening with me, we decided that we'd go to the doctors and see if they could do anything to help. My doctor had to refer me to a Gender Clinic, so that I could see some specialist doctors who are properly trained in this area. I had to wait a long time on the waiting list, but I finally got my appointment at the clinic.

The clinic talks to me and my mum and my dad. Sometimes we have sessions together and sometimes we have them separately. This is really good because it's given me the chance to talk about how I feel about myself with people that I trust, and it also means that my mum and dad have people to talk to.

The clinic is where I met one of my best friends, Amy. She hasn't been going to the clinic as long as I have because she didn't have a teacher who could help her like I did. She was a little bit older when she had to tell her dad that something didn't feel right and for a long time he wouldn't listen to her, and so she got sadder and sadder and didn't want to do anything or take part in things at school. Eventually he took her to the doctor and she told them everything, and the doctor referred her to the clinic so that she had someone to talk to and so did her dad.

As Amy's a little bit older than me, she started on hormone blockers before I did. Hormone blockers are a type of treatment that stops you from going through the puberty you were assigned at birth. It's reversible and it can stop you experiencing anything horrible while you try to work out what you want to do next. My dad says it's a really good thing because it means that I don't have to make any super fast decisions, or feel like I'm being rushed into anything.

The best thing about hormone blockers is that if I change my mind then they won't hurt my body. I don't think that that's going to happen for me, but Dad says that they give me a little bit of time to get more comfortable with the body that I'm growing into. Amy decided that she wanted to go on hormone blockers, so that her voice wouldn't break and she wouldn't develop an Adam's apple. Nobody at the clinic makes you feel rushed and I really like that because sometimes it's really exhausting to think about how big the world is and how little I am. Every day I get a little bit more comfortable in my own skin, and I've started to think that if it feels right for me then I'm going to want to take testosterone at 16. This means I'll be able to go through boy puberty at the same time as other boys in my class. My friend Tobi doesn't think that they want to go through hormones, but might have top surgery so that they don't have breasts, because they just don't feel comfortable in their body as it is, but they don't feel binary about gender. Not all of us at the clinic have the same answers to the questions that we're asked, but we're always told that that's okay, and we can talk about it with other people and learn as we grow. That matters a lot because it can be really hard to have so many questions, and we're trying just to work out our own answers and whatever makes us feel best and there's no map for us to understand how this works.

The clinic waits and talks to you a lot before you have to decide if this is something that you want to do. Once you're on hormone blockers, there are really two directions you can go in when you're 18. You can either stop taking the hormone blockers and your body will carry on the way it was going to, or you can change and take hormone replacement therapy to help your body become the right body for you.

Going to the doctors isn't just about being on medicine though! One of the best things about going to the clinic is that I get to see my friends, and we get to talk to each other about what it's like to be trans. The doctors are really nice to us and nobody ever forces us into thinking or feeling a certain way. This is really important because it can feel really scary to not feel good in your own body and it's nice to know that people are there to help."

"One of the things that we talk about a lot in the clinic is how to be careful with language. When we had people from the clinic come into my school to talk, this was also one of the things that they talked to my teachers about.

The first thing that happens in a group is that we introduce ourselves and tell people the pronouns we'd like people to call us. This is really important because you can't tell what somebody would like to be called just by looking at them, and it's a really good habit to get into. Amy's pronouns are she or her. My friend Sam's pronouns are they or them, because Sam is non-binary. Leigh's pronouns are xe, and xe are gender fluid. Sometimes we talk about other pronouns that you might be able to use, like ze or zir, or xie. There are lots of different pronouns and that's a really good thing because it's about finding what makes you most comfortable.

It's also really important to make sure that we use the right names for people. I make sure people know that Kit is my name, and it would be really good if they could call me he or him. I know that sometimes I might be the first trans person that people have met, and that they don't always know what to do. It feels bad when somebody gets my pronouns wrong, but I always correct them and then we can move on. It doesn't have to be a big deal! It feels horrible when somebody makes a fuss about not being able to remember because it makes me feel like I'm inconveniencing them or being difficult when I'm really just trying to be myself.

One of the things that I find really funny is that when I'm walking my dog, Pickle, sometimes people will think that Pickle is a girl. When I tell them that he's a boy, they apologise and get his pronoun right. I wish people in everyday life would be like that with me sometimes, it doesn't feel like it should be so difficult!"

"One of the things that's great about living in the UK is that everybody is protected by something called The Equality Act. This was made in 2010 to make sure that people don't suffer because they're a bit different. It's a list of nine ways you can't be horrible to somebody.

The nine protected areas are age, disability, gender reassignment, marriage and civil partnership, pregnancy and maternity, race, religion or belief, sex and sexual orientation. Being transgender comes under gender reassignment, and it means that if you are trans then nobody can stop you getting a job, or going to school, or treat you differently than they would if you weren't trans.

This means that by law, schools are supposed to be safe spaces for all students, and it meant that the school could do things to help me without worrying that they were breaking any laws. In fact, the Act makes sure that people know that schools are one of the places that The Equality Act has to apply."

"Once I started to call myself Kit and decided to come out properly, I was a bit worried about what school would be like. I'm the first student in the school who has ever gone through transition and I was worried that people would be mean or would say horrible things to me. My parents came to the school to talk to my head teacher. I decided I didn't want to go to a different school because I really like my school and I didn't want to be in a new place away from my friends, so there were lots of things that we needed to do to make sure that it could go smoothly.

I had to officially change my name on the school records, and the school had to make sure that they kept my other documents somewhere private. My head teacher asked me if it was okay that the other teachers know what it is that I'm going through, and we decided together that we would tell all of the teachers.

My head teacher also invited a trainer into the school to talk about gender identity, and give some workshops so that the teachers could talk easily with all of us. A lot of people don't know that your gender identity is really different from who you'd like to go out with.

One of the things that we had to work out was how I was going to come out to the other people at school. We decided that after the summer holidays, I would come back as Kit, and let everybody know who I really am. I was really nervous to go back that day but what I didn't know was that my teacher had asked everybody in my class to make a 'Welcome Back, Kit!' sign. Everybody also wore stickers saying what their pronouns were, and we talked about all of our favourite things and what we wanted to do or be when we grew up. I was really happy, and at lunchtime my friends made sure that I had a seat and that I was happy to be back, and everyone was really supportive. It made me less scared to be in school and I didn't feel like I stuck out for bad reasons.

My school also bought some library books, and for the first time I could read stories that were about people like me. Other people read the books too, and at first it was a little bit scary because I didn't want everybody to point me out and think that I'm strange, but because the school gave everybody a chance to talk about things it meant that nobody was afraid or worried about saying something wrong.

This was really important for me when it came to really simple things like going to the bathroom and using the changing room for sports. The school looked at the toilets they had and decided that they would mark some of them as gender neutral, so that anybody can use them. They told me I didn't have to use them like this, that I could use the boys' toilets if I wanted to but that the decision was mine, and that felt really good because it meant that I wasn't being singled out.

The trainer also talked about ways that we could talk about gender in class. So instead of splitting up our class into 'girls' and 'boys', we'd be split up by numbers or colours or heights. This meant that when we were asked to do something, I didn't feel like I was weird or different, and it also helped other people in my class too. They also looked at school uniforms and decided that it was silly to have 'boy' clothes and 'girl' clothes, so the school changed the rules to say that people could wear the uniform that they wanted to wear and that they'd be most comfortable in. Some parents were a bit concerned at first about what this might mean, because it's a new thing and my dad says that sometimes people get a little bit wary about change, but the school didn't make a big deal about it."

"Sometimes it's easy to forget that it's not always great for everyone in the world. There are places in the world right now where other people get really angry about what people want to do with their own bodies, and think that there's something wrong with who we are as people. These people refuse to call transgender people by their names, or by the right pronouns. When somebody does this, we call it misgendering, and it's a horrible thing to do to anybody.

Of course, sometimes it happens by accident! It's still not nice when somebody uses the wrong name or the wrong pronoun, but when that happens I understand. Usually I just correct them and we move on because I know it was a mistake.

Sometimes when I do that, the person gets a little bit upset. That makes me sad because they don't need to tell me all of the reasons that remembering is hard for them. I understand because I'm still a person and sometimes I still make mistakes. All I need them to do is to move on.

When I first started coming out, sometimes I got my own pronouns wrong! Because I was so used to my old name and my old pronouns, it felt really strange to start using new ones. This is something that can happen to a lot of trans people and it doesn't mean that they're not 'trans enough' or aren't 'real' trans people. It's just something that you need to get used to, just like all people have to get used to things!"

"That's been the most important thing for me to remember – it isn't that I'm a transgender person, it's that I'm just a person. This means that I was a lot of things, not just this one thing, and I'm *still* all of those things. So I still really love climbing trees, and reading books, and singing songs, and drawing pictures. I love having a cuddle with my mum and dad, and watching cartoons, and my happiest thing in life is to spend time with Pickle every day, because animals don't care about what gender you are, they just care about who you are on the inside.

When I get frustrated, I just have to remember that things are happening and changing. In the newspapers or the news, people aren't careful. They might say something rude about a celebrity or a famous person who's talking about transgender things, and they won't necessarily realise that I have eyes and ears and can hear too.

The same is true when people tell me that I'm just a kid, because I know my body better than anybody else does. Most of the time when it comes to the thoughtless things that people say, I'm getting better at ignoring them. I know who I am, and I feel bad for them because they miss out on amazing things when they don't take the time to get to know other people!"

HOW OTHER PEOPLE CAN HELP

A note on language: I have elected not to use the + or * after trans, as trans is commonly understood as an embracing umbrella term. Throughout the guide, I refer to trans or those experiencing gender variance. Absolutely no discrimination is meant by my use of these terms, and they are intended to be as far reaching and encompassing as is linguistically possible.

In the past two years, there has been a significant increase in the number of young people who have come out as transgender or gender queer. As society becomes more accepting, and with the increase in conversations about gender, this rise is set to continue. A conservative estimate suggests that 1% of the population identifies as trans, although there is currently a huge lag between the reality of trans identity in Britain and any demographic reports.

It's natural that children are becoming aware of their identities younger, and are starting to ask questions of gender, regardless of how they identify. This means that adults need to be prepared to have these conversations in a way that is helpful, and avoids the risk of causing any harm or psychological damage.

GENDER NON-CONFORMING BEHAVIOUR

First, it's important to remember that there is a difference between gender non-conforming behaviour and gender identity. When we talk about gender non-conforming behaviour, we are referring to the breaking down of societal stereotypes of what it "means" to be a man or boy, and what it "means" to be a woman or girl, and only splitting things into these two categories (or what we call "the binary"). This is particularly significant for young people who learn through a process of mimicry the ways that they are expected to behave. The freedom for a girl to like sports, the colour blue, or for boys to wear skirts or enjoy cooking is a vitally important one – but this may or may not have anything to do with their gender identity. It is accepted that young people could, and should, experiment with what they enjoy, and conversations that free a child from the expectations of stereotypes are important for all children, not just those who identify as transgender.

There are ways that an adult can foster an environment where a child feels safe to explore their identity:

- engage in conversations about why it is that we stereotype

- be flexible in your understandings of what it is to be a boy or a girl

- resist the urge to limit a child's behaviour

- use the same language to talk about boys and girls

- reduce the child's anxiety about ways they might be different

- be creative and stress the importance of being an individual

- don't break things into a binary of either/or but spectrum

- keep an eye on conversations around the child

- support making and keeping friends

- reinforce the importance of enjoyment over conforming

- default to the gender neutral, rather than the masculine or feminine.

All children deserve the right to express their identity in whatever way makes them comfortable, and it is the role of an adult to ensure that they feel empowered about their place and identity within the larger framework of society.

TRANSGENDER CHILDREN

The experience of transgender children is a different experience from just being different from the gender stereotypes. Portrayal in the press suggests that children are always aware of their gender identity and struggle with it from an early age, and in some cases, this is true. From the development of their language skills, some children understand that their gender identity and the gender that they were assigned at birth are different from one another. For others, this may happen at any period in their lives – right through into adulthood. It is important to realise that there is no set route that being trans takes – there is no such thing as being trans enough, there is no one way to be trans. Just like everybody else, transgender people are individuals with nuanced needs that change and differ on a case by case basis.

That being said, non-conforming behaviour can sometimes be a way that young children attempt to manifest their understanding of their gender identity. By encouraging a child to experiment freely, it can help alleviate any concerns that the child might have about being accepted, or ease their worries about not being "good enough". Some children may be very comfortable in their process, and may find elements of transition a natural process. However, the process of working out their gender identity, or feeling a change in their gender identity, can be something that some children need help with. Some signs that a child may need additional support include:

- issues with concentration

- difficulty with schoolwork, and deteriorating grades

- complete investment in schoolwork to the exclusion of all else

- reluctance to use toilets at school

- reluctance to do physical exercise, especially if it is seen as stereotypically "male" or "female",

or an unwillingness to use gendered changing
rooms

- missing school, constant sickness

- self harm or suicide attempts

- being bullied, often targeted homophobic
bullying

- having very few friends.

LISTENING AND TALKING

Whether or not your child, or the children in your
classroom, identify as transgender, it's increasingly
likely that they will know somebody who identifies
as trans, and therefore important that this is
usualised as readily as possible.

Some children will be very self-aware and will
want to discuss the issues they are having with
their gender. There is no one-size-fits-all approach
to caring for those whose gender identity is
different from how they were assigned at birth, so
it's important to make sure that first and foremost
you are seeing the person, rather than a perceived
"problem".

Some young people, and their families, may
benefit from peer support to give them a safe,
understanding space in which to discuss their

issues and to meet other people with no demands placed on them as to how they might handle transition going forwards. GIRES, the Gender Identity Research and Education Society, is a charity which sponsors research and education on gender identity.

This can also be particularly important for parents and carers of young people who are initially less supportive of their child's gender identity. Groups such as Gendered Intelligence, the community interest company who advocate for understanding gender diversity in creative ways, run online forums specifically for families to access, where people can share stories with other families in similar positions.

If working with parents and carers, it's important that a teacher remember they are representing the interests of the young person and, where there is conflict, not necessarily their parents. Confidential information shouldn't be shared with anybody else without the express permission of the child or young person unless there is a safeguarding issue.

SELF HARM AND SUICIDE
Current statistics suggest that young trans people are some of the most vulnerable in society, and face a much higher risk of self harm and

suicide than others. This is true across the board for LGBTQ identified children. The 2014 Youth Chances report, released by METRO in collaboration with Ergo Consulting and the University of Greenwich, found that those who identify as a member of the LGBTQ community face higher levels of discrimination, bullying, verbal and physical violence.

Sixty-one per cent of the whole sample reported name calling because they were LGBTQ or *people thought they were.* This usualising of homophobic, biphobic and transphobic bullying is often interlinked – perceptions that a "boy" is behaving "like a girl" can often mean that a child is bullied for this perceived transgression.

According to the report, the overwhelming message from young people is that schools can and should do much more, and that they are being failed by the systems which have been put in place to help them. One in two young trans identified people will have seriously considered suicide, with one in three young trans identified people having attempted it.

The act of denying a young person access to their identity or the freedom to explore it can also have seriously negative repercussions later on in life, including serious issues with self harm, suicidal thoughts, and continuing depression.

SCHOOL

When it comes to helping young people, the school environment is often the arena in which young people will feel more open about talking or exploring their gender issues. All schools need to work towards being an embracing, understanding environment. Academic research has shown that a whole school approach towards educating about trans issues, as well as ensuring that issues of transphobia are dealt with immediately and firmly, is a way of starting to minimise the stress that young trans people face while at school.

In the UK, organisations such as Educate & Celebrate offer an Ofsted recognised, holistic approach to LGBTQ education which engages students, teachers, parents, governors and support staff in ensuring that everybody is equipped and comfortable to deal with any issues that may be encountered. This takes the onus away from PSHE lessons, and instead allows for acceptance that all people within the school environment are treated equally and fairly.

There are many ways that a school can make sure that the community is aware of the commitment to eradicating transphobia and supporting trans and gender variant young people.

This can include:

- marking trans day of visibility and trans day of remembrance

- an anti-bullying week focus on transphobia

- covering the issues in LGBT History Month

- providing information in classes, including PSHE, about gender identity

- workshop days and inviting outside speakers.

While there may be out and openly trans identified children in school, there are also going to be cases where a school has a trans identified student and their identity is not known to the school. It is the legal obligation of the school to make sure that this information is protected and that a young person's identity is kept private unless it is the person's wish that it should be known.

THE EQUALITY ACT

The introduction of The Equality Act (2010) means that schools must be prepared to eliminate homophobic, biphobic and transphobic bullying, as one of the nine protected characteristics.

Currently, trans identified and gender variant people are protected by the characteristic "gender reassignment", and schools are explicitly mentioned within the Act. This means that it is against the law for schools to discriminate against trans identified or gender variant pupils, and will have to factor in gender as part of the obligations to the Equality Act.

"Gender reassignment" is defined in The Equality Act as applying to anyone who is undergoing, has undergone or is proposing to undergo a process (or part of a process) of reassigning their sex by changing physiological or other attributes. While this may seem vague, it essentially covers anybody who may choose to socially and/or medically transition.

When it comes to safeguarding, there are absolutely no issues under child protection or safeguarding laws specific to trans identified and gender variant young people. So, for example, there is nothing that would stop trans identified children and young people from using the changing rooms or toilets which reflect their gender identity.

Many schools are now taking the important steps to incorporate gender neutral facilities within the school environment, which is to be specifically commended as it eases the presumption of the binary for those who identify outside of the binary, and can ease concerns pupils may have about using the "right" or "wrong" facilities.

Trans identified and gender questioning pupils and students have the right to dress in a manner consistent with their gender identity or gender expression. By providing a choice of approved items of uniform and allowing pupils and students to choose what they wish to wear, schools will allow for regulated structure but without exclusion. Indeed, many female born students prefer to wear trousers to school or may have religious or faith based reasons for doing so.

Depending on the individual and their choices for transition, they might choose to begin dressing in the clothes associated with their chosen gender, and this may include making a choice about school uniform. This can be a huge, early step towards social transition, and the pupils are making themselves visibly more different from many of the school community. This means that a student may require extra support at this time. Again, training all members of staff to ensure they know how to effectively communicate with and on behalf of the whole school community is vitally important. Addressing policies is a significant step in the right direction, and schools should consider listing uniform items simply as items of clothing, rather than codifying clothes into "boy" clothes and "girl" clothes. This means that the uniform for the school can be upheld, while still respecting a student's identity.

CONFIDENTIALITY

When it comes to issues of confidentiality, all people have the right to privacy, and this includes keeping your trans status or gender identity private. Nobody is entitled to information about a young person's transgender status, their legal name, or gender assigned at birth. This right to privacy extends across all arenas, including in school, and staff should not discuss a student's transgender status without the express permission of the student – the same is true when talking about a trans student at school to friends or other people outside of the school. The size of the trans community, and people's curiosity means that even the mention of a trans student can out a student without their permission.

When a child or young person initially discloses their status, it is important to talk to them about confidentiality and who they want you to share the information with. Trans identified and gender variant pupils have the right to discuss their identity without fear or concern – this may also change through the course of their transition. When contacting the parent or carer, school personnel should use the student's legal name and the pronoun corresponding to the student's gender assigned at birth unless the pupils, student, parent, or carer has specified otherwise, as the home environment may not always be supportive.

HBT BULLYING AND WHAT TO DO

When it comes to homophobic, biphobic and transphobic bullying, it can be difficult to separate the strands as the language is often interchangeable. What is significant is that trans identified and gender variant young people are vulnerable to bullying which can contribute significant stress to an already emotionally charged situation.

Transphobic bullying can come from all areas of society, including pupils, students, parents, or any members of staff, either directly or indirectly. The reinforcement of gender stereotypes and placing judgement on those who are seen to be "transgressing" can be actively harmful, and often people will not be aware that they are speaking to a trans person when passing sweeping statements about those inside or outside of the school community.

Schools must make a commitment through curriculum, assemblies and the whole school environment to challenge these sweeping assumptions in order to make sure that the learning environment is safe and embracing for all young people. Following on from this, all transphobic bullying and incidents need to be specifically recorded and treated with the utmost seriousness.

If a transphobic incident occurs and the member of staff knows that the child or young person identifies as trans but is not out or open about it, they must make sure to challenge the bullying behaviour without labelling the pupil. There may also be times when transphobic bullying has wider safeguarding implications or involves criminal behaviour, and in these cases schools need to engage the appropriate safeguarding agencies and/or the police.

LANGUAGE

Communication is key, and one of the easiest ways to reinforce the respect for trans identity and gender variance is through how we speak to one another.

Respecting a change of pronouns is a great way to ensure that a trans or gender variant young person feels respected and supported in their identity. It's also important to be consistent with the use of pronouns and names.

Some trans identified and gender variant young people may wish to change their name to make it in line with their chosen gender identity. Although they may not have changed their name legally, individuals have the right to choose the name by which they are known to staff, friends and family.

Members of the school community should strive to use the preferred pronoun for all students, and in encouraging the whole school to consider how they use language, asking all people to specify their preferred pronouns is a great, inclusive way to break assumptions about how to refer to anybody. This includes on visitor sign in forms, and on forms where options of a title are given – not just to students, but also to parents.

The use of language in general throughout the school should show a commitment to breaking the sense of a binary, and veer away from the idea that there are only two genders. Using language such as "boys and girls" or "ladies and gents" is not only exclusionary to trans identified and gender variant young people, but subtly reinforces that gender is a significant difference about behaviour patterns. It may instead be preferable to group students into classes, or houses, or pupils.

This isn't to suggest that gender is insignificant, or an important part of many people's identities, but simply ensures that, when trying to make time-saving gestures, members of staff are not excluding those who do not see themselves as male or female, or make assumptions about someone's gender identity because of how they appear. While it may feel a little uncomfortable or unusual at first, once again the whole school approach quickly usualises the language.

GENDER CLINICS

While not all young people will choose to undergo medical transition, it does help to know some of the steps that are available for young people.

Medical treatment is in a system of steps that may or may not naturally progress, and is highly specific to the person choosing to go through it. It can include:

- psychological assessment and counselling, initially with a Child and Adolescent Mental Health Services (CAMHS) worker who may refer to a Gender Identity Clinic

- medication known as hormone blockers, which essentially pauses the body's attempt to go through puberty until the young person has decided if they want this, or would prefer hormone replacement therapy

- hormones to masculinise or feminise the body – usually not until the age of 16

- surgical intervention – usually not until over 18 years old.

The process of transition is a long, slow one which involves a lot of time on waiting lists, particularly going through the NHS. The initial stages of transition can be daunting, no matter how certain the young person is, and they might need access to counselling to support them through their time, and to ensure that the family also has the support mechanisms in place.

Mermaids is a UK-based charity which offers support and assistance for young people and families of young people who are trans identified. It includes resources and information for parents, teachers, and many other groups.

When it comes to dealing with gender variance, an open and inclusive practice can make the school a safer environment for all students, not just those who are questioning their gender identity, or those going through transition. In essence, the most important thing to remember is that the student is still a student – with all the complex needs of every other young person their own age. While an important aspect of their identity, identifying as trans or gender variant is a facet of a whole, brilliant, complicated identity and the young person should be celebrated for that.

FURTHER GUIDANCE AND SUPPORT GROUPS

There are, of course, many groups that operate around the country that deal with LGBTQ help and assistance, and the following list is meant neither to be definitive nor exclusionary. The following resources offer trans-specific advice, teaching guides or reading lists, or offer links to places where you can find more specific information.

Educate & Celebrate
www.educateandcelebrate.org
Educate & Celebrate is an Ofsted recognised Best Practice Programme that gives staff, students, parents and governors the confidence and strategies to implement an LGBT+Inclusive curriculum to successfully eradicate homophobia, biphobia and transphobia from our schools and communities.

Gendered Intelligence
www.genderedintelligence.co.uk
A community interest company that delivers arts programmes, creative workshops, mentoring, training and youth group sessions to trans youth (under the age of 25).

GenderJam

www.genderjam.org.uk

A charity for the young transgender community in Northern Ireland, based in Belfast and Newry, bringing young trans, non-binary, questioning and intersex people together to create resources to help the community in Northern Ireland.

GIRES Gender Identity Research and Education Society

www.gires.org.uk

National body that examines the science around gender and transgender individuals; produces a wide range of resources for schools and other public bodies, including a toolkit on combating transphobic bullying and an e-learning package.

Mermaids

www.mermaidsuk.org.uk

National charity that connects and supports young trans people and their families.

The Tavistock and Portman Clinic

www.tavistockandportman.nhs.uk

For children and young people (up to the age of 18) and their families experiencing difficulties in the development of their gender identity, including children unhappy with their biological sex.

The Beaumont Society

www.beaumontsociety.org.uk

National society that supports mainly M2F trans people and their families and friends.

UK Trans Info

www.uktrans.info

A national charity focused on improving the lives of trans and non-binary people in the UK.

GLOSSARY

Assigned gender
The gender you were assigned at birth and raised as

(C)AFAB
(Coercively) Assigned female at birth

(C)AMAB
(Coercively) Assigned male at birth

Cisgender
Somebody whose gender identity is the same as their assigned gender

FTM/Transman/Transmasculine/Transsexual man/ Transgender man
Someone assigned female at birth but who identifies as male

Gender
How a person feels in regards to male/female/neither/ both/other. A process of recognising one's identity

Genderqueer/Gender fluid/Gender non-binary
A gender variant or diverse person whose gender identity is neither male nor female, is between or beyond genders, a combination of male and female, or who identifies beyond the gender binary of "male" and "female"

Gender dysphoria

A recognised medical term which refers to the discomfort of being perceived and living as your assigned sex

Gender euphoria

A term which refers to the joy when recognised as one's gender identity

GIC

Gender Identity Clinic

Intersex

A term for a variety of conditions in which a person is born with a reproductive or sexual anatomy that doesn't seem to fit the typical definitions of male and female

LGBTQ

Lesbian, Gay, Bisexual, Transgender and Queer. The 'Q' can sometimes also mean questioning

MTF/Transwoman/Transfeminine/Transsexual woman/Transgender woman

Someone assigned as male at birth who identifies as female

Outing

To make public somebody's gender status without their consent (also used when someone has made public someone's sexual orientation without their consent)

Pansexual/Panromantic

A sexual or romantic attraction towards people of all gender identities including those that don't fit into a gender binary

Passing/blending

Being seen or perceived as the gender you present yourself as, e.g. a male identifying person being read as male

Pronouns

How we refer to people: he/him/his; she/her/hers; they/them/theirs (the singular they for gender neutral); sie/sie/sie, hir/hir/hirs, zie/zie/zies

Sexual orientation

Attraction to people, i.e. homosexual/hetereosexual/bisexual/pansexual, etc.

To gender

To assign someone a gender based on how you perceive them; to assign something a gender based on societal expectations, e.g. giving something that is pink a typically "female" name

Trans

An umbrella term which can be used to describe people who may be:

- transgender
- transsexual
- both male and female
- neither male nor female
- androgynous
- a third gender
- someone whose has a gender identity that there is not currently a word for

Transphobia

The irrational fear, hatred, abuse etc. of trans people or those who do not conform to traditional gender norms

Transvestite/Cross dresser

A person, typically a cisgendered man, who derives pleasure from dressing in clothes societally determined as 'female'